worthy

MEDITATIONS
ON THE
LAMB OF GOD

CREATED BY

jeff rouse

Engravings by Living Stone Music, Nashville, TN.

FOR HE ALONE IS

As the canticle of the New Testament comes to an end on the Isle of Patmos with the Revelations of the Apostle John, we are given an almost inconceivable glimpse of eternal praise.

FOR HE ALONE IS

worthy

Then I looked, and I heard the voice of many angels around the throne, the living creatures, and the elders; and the number of them was ten thousand times ten thousand, and thousands of thousands, saying with a loud voice: "Worthy is the Lamb who was slain to receive power and riches and wisdom, and strength and honor and glory and blessing!" And every creature which is in Heaven and on the earth and under the earth and such as are in the sea, and all that are in them, I heard saying: "Blessing and honor and glory and power be to Him who sits on the throne, and to the Lamb, forever and ever!" Revelation 5:11-13 NIV

FOR HE ALONE IS

worthy

The endless, glorious, cacophony of praise and worship described here can also manifest itself in the quiet meditations of the heart. This selection of familiar songs, exquisitely arranged by Jay Rouse for solo piano, was created to allow the pianist and audience to meditate on those things that Christ alone is worthy to receive... power... riches... wisdom... strength... honor... glory... blessing... Worthy is the Lamb!

CHRIST THE

MIGHTY IS OUR GOD

My salvation and my honor depend on God; He is my mighty rock, my refuge. (Psalm 62:7 NIV)

Words and Music by
EUGENE GRECO, GERRIT GUSTAFSON
and DON MOEN
Arr. by Jay Rouse

Brightly, steady tempo ♩ = 120

18 *like the beginning*

21

25

29

33

sub. mp

36

mf

maintain steady tempo

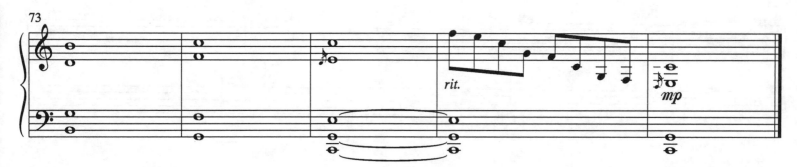

WHAT A MIGHTY GOD WE SERVE

Our God, the great, mighty and awesome God. (Nehemiah 9:32 NIV)

AUTHOR UNKNOWN
Arr. by Jay Rouse

8

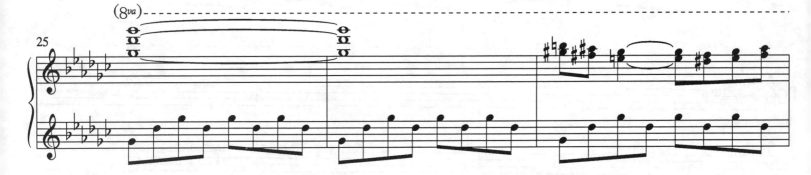

O FOR A THOUSAND TONGUES TO SING (Words by Charles Wesley/Music by Carl G. Gläser)

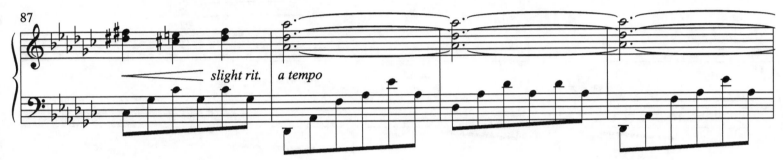

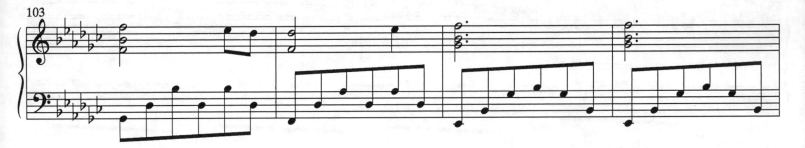

MORE PRECIOUS THAN SILVER

You are my Lord; apart from You I have no good thing. (Psalm 16:2 NIV)

Words and Music by
LYNN DESHAZO
Arr. by Jay Rouse

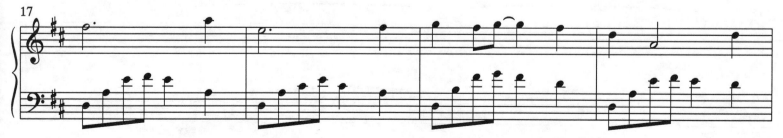

16

like the beginning

I WORSHIP YOU, ALMIGHTY GOD

You alone are the Lord. You made the heavens, even the highest heavens, and all their starry host, the earth and all that is on it, the seas and all that is in them. You give life to everything, and the multitudes of Heaven worship You. (Nehemiah 9:6 NIV)

Words and Music by
SONDRA CORBETT WOOD
Arr. by Jay Rouse

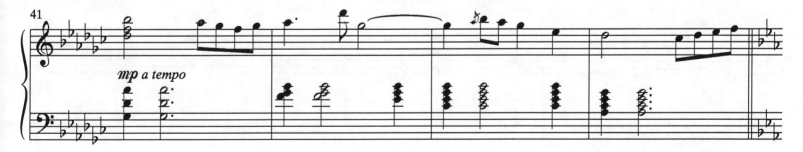

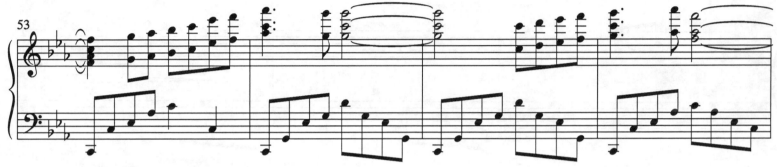

THOU ART WORTHY

You are worthy, our Lord and God, to receive glory and honor and power. (Revelation 4:11 NIV)

Words and Music by
PAULINE MICHAEL MILLS
Arr. by Jay Rouse

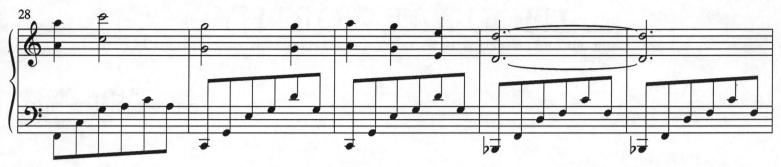

GIVE THANKS

The Lord is my strength and my shield; my heart trusts in Him, and I am helped.
My heart leaps for joy and I will give thanks to Him in song. (Psalm 28:7 NIV)

Words and Music by
HENRY SMITH
Arr. by Jay Rouse

Slowly with great feeling

Faster, in a slow two ♩ = 96

THINK ABOUT HIS LOVE

As high as the heavens above the earth, so great is His love for those who fear Him. (Psalm 103:11 NIV)

Words and Music by
WALT HARRAH
Arr. by Jay Rouse

YOU ARE CROWNED WITH MANY CROWNS

On His head are many crowns. (Revelation 19:12 NIV)

Words and Music by
JOHN SELLERS
Arr. by Jay Rouse

With energy ♩ = 132

CROWN HIM WITH MANY CROWNS (Words by Matthew Bridges/Music by George J. Elvey)

a little broader

BE EXALTED, O GOD

Great is Your love. Be exalted, O God, above the heavens. (Psalm 57:10-11)

Words and Music by
BRENT CHAMBERS
Arr. by Jay Rouse

Like the beginning ♩ = 84

GLORIFY THY NAME

I will praise You, O Lord my God, with all my heart; I will glorify Your name forever. (Psalm 86:12 NIV)

Words and Music by
DONNA ADKINS
Arr. by Jay Rouse

BLESSED BE THE NAME OF THE LORD

The crowds that went ahead of Him and those that followed shouted, "Hosanna to the Son of David!"
"Blessed is He Who comes in the name of the Lord!" "Hosanna in the highest!" (Matthew 21:9 NIV)

Words and Music by
DON MOEN
Arr. by Jay Rouse

JOY OF MY DESIRE

Whom have I in Heaven but You? And earth has nothing I desire besides You. (Psalm 73:25 NIV)

Words and Music by
JENNIFER RANDOLPH
Arr. by Jay Rouse

index

PRODUCT INFORMATION

Piano Book 000768 16106 7
Listening Cassette 000768 16104 3
Listening CD 000768 16102 9

All product available from your favorite music supplier or directly from Integrity Music at 1-800-239-7000.
Visit our web site at www.integinc.com.
The numbers in the boxed area indicate the product number to be used when placing an order directly with Integrity Music.